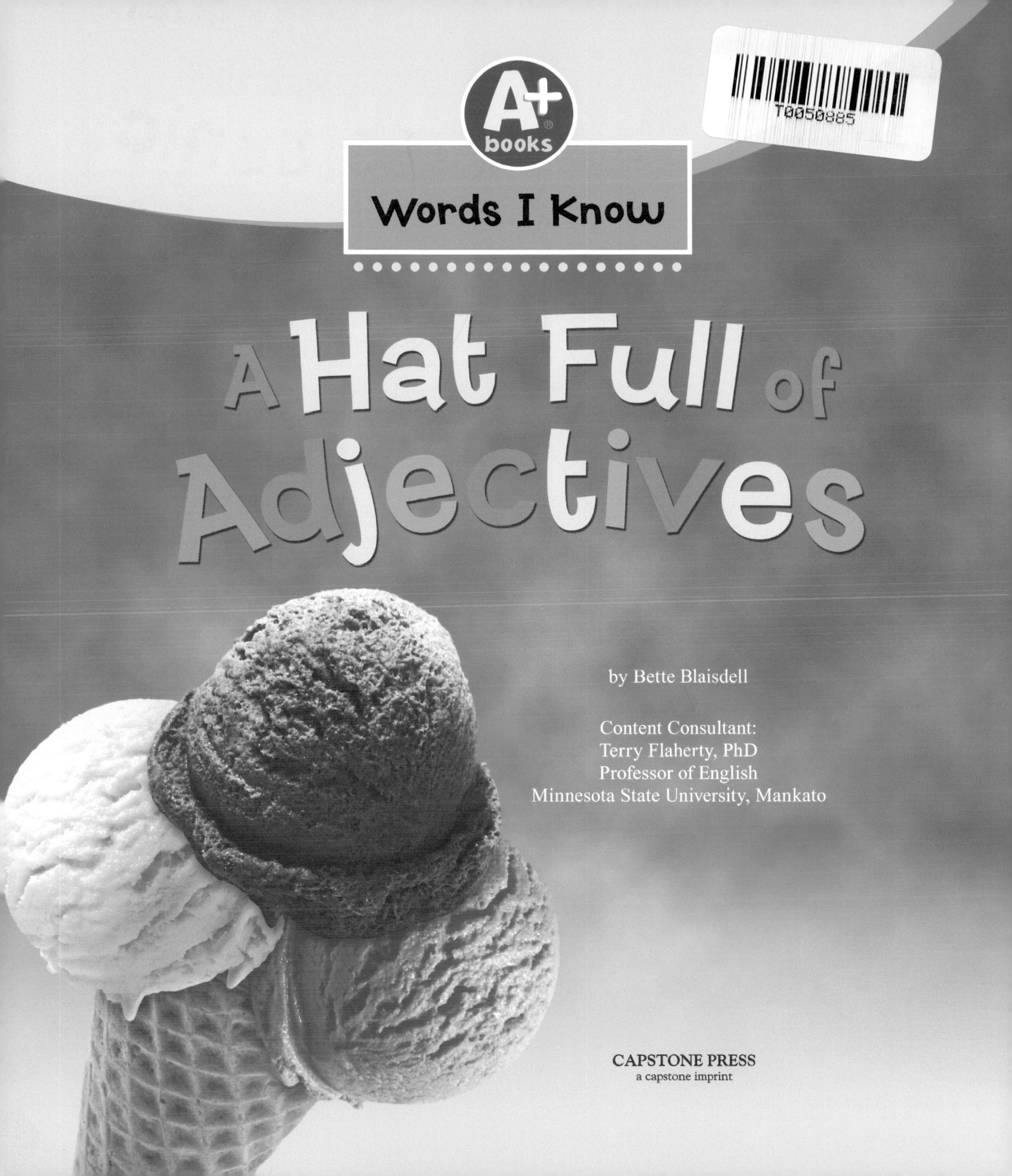
A+ books
Words I Know
A Hat Full of Adjectives
by Bette Blaisdell
Content Consultant:
Terry Flaherty, PhD
Professor of English
Minnesota State University, Mankato
CAPSTONE PRESS
a capstone imprint
T0050885

A+ Books are published by Capstone Press,
1710 Roe Crest Drive, North Mankato, Minnesota 56003
www.capstonepub.com

Copyright © 2014 by Capstone Press, a Capstone imprint. All rights reserved. No part of this publication may be reproduced in whole or in part, or stored in a retrieval system, or transmitted in any form or by any means, electronic, mechanical, photocopying, recording, or otherwise, without written permission of the publisher.

Library of Congress Cataloging-in-Publication Data
Blaisdell, Bette.
A hat full of adjectives / by Bette Blaisdell.
pages cm.—(A+ books. Words i know)
Summary: "Full-color photographs and rhyming text introduce and define a variety of adjectives"—Provided by publisher.
ISBN 978-1-4765-3937-9 (library binding)
ISBN 978-1-4765-5097-8 (paperback)
ISBN 978-1-4765-5942-1 (eBook PDF)
1. English language—adjective—Juvenile literature. I. Title.
PE1241.B48 2014
425'.5—dc23 2013035671

Editorial Credits
Jill Kalz, editor; Juliette Peters, designer; Svetlana Zhurkin, media researcher; Kathy McColley, production specialist

Photo Credits
iStockphotos: wdstock, 8; Shutterstock: 2xSamara, 10, AKaiser, 2–3, 4–5 (back), 32, Andrey Arkusha, 22 (top), Anneka, cover, Annette Shaff, 28 (top), Bernhard Richter, 15 (bottom), bikeriderlondon, 24 (bottom), Brocreative, 4 (bottom), buruhtan, 26, Chen WS, 22 (bottom), Dan Breckwoldt, 5 (right), Danny Smythe, 27 (top right), Denis Trofimov, 13 (top), Dusan Zidar, 24 (top), Elena Schweitzer, 18 (top), Elenamiv, 21 (bottom), Florin Stana, 25 (top), Givaga, 19 (middle), GVictoria, 5 (left), Igor Terekhov, 14 (bottom left), Ivonne Wierink, 6–7, Jan S., 12–13 (back), Jean-Edouard Rozey, 18 (bottom), Jerry Horbert, 28 (bottom), JonMilnes, 25 (bottom), Joy Fera, 16 (bottom), Kenishirotie, 27 (bottom), Kokhanchikov, 29, kostrez, 9 (bottom), Leena Robinson, 4 (top), M. Unal Ozmen, 1, Madlen, 27 (top left), mexrix, 14 (bottom right), mycola, 20 (bottom), Nailia Schwarz, 9 (top), naluwan, 11 (top), Norman Chan, 12 (right), OLJ Studio, 12 (left), Paulo M. F. Pires, 16 (top), Photo Fun, 14 (top), Rob Hainer, 23 (bottom), Rohit Seth, 21 (top), Rosli Othman, 11 (bottom), saiko3p, 19 (top), Sanjay Deva, 23 (top), Sergey Novikov, 20 (top), Steven Russell Smith Photos, 19 (bottom), Svetlana Valoueva, 13 (bottom), Varina and Jay Patel, 15 (top), Vilainecrevette, 17, Zurijeta, 30–31

Note to Parents, Teachers, and Librarians
This Words I Know book uses full-color photographs and a nonfiction format to introduce the concept of language and parts of speech. *A Hat Full of Adjectives* is designed to be read aloud to a pre-reader or to be read independently by an early reader. Photographs help listeners and early readers understand the text and concepts discussed. The book encourages further learning by including the following sections: Table of Contents, Read More, and Internet Sites. Early readers may need assistance using these features.

Printed in the United States 5029

Table of Contents

What's an Adjective? 4
Beyond the Rainbow 6
Size It Up 8
How Do You Feel? 10
Your Listening Ears 12
Not the Same 14
What's Your Speed? 16
By the Numbers 18
Weather Report 20
Who Are You? 22
The Shape of Things 24
Taste Test 26
Keep in Touch 28
What a Day! 30

Read More 32
Internet Sites 32

What's an Adjective?

How many kids are on the swing? *Three*! What kind of ice cream does Maya like? *Peppermint*! Which dog is Luke's? The *spotted* dog!

You've just met some adjectives.

An **adjective** is a part of speech that describes a person, place, or thing. It adds detail.

Adjectives may tell how something looks, smells, tastes, feels, or sounds. They may answer these questions: How many? How big? What kind? Which? Adjectives usually come before the objects they describe in a sentence.

What silly, fluffy adjectives will you pull out of *your* hat?

Beyond the Rainbow

You've seen red, blue, yellow, and green.
How many other colors have you seen?

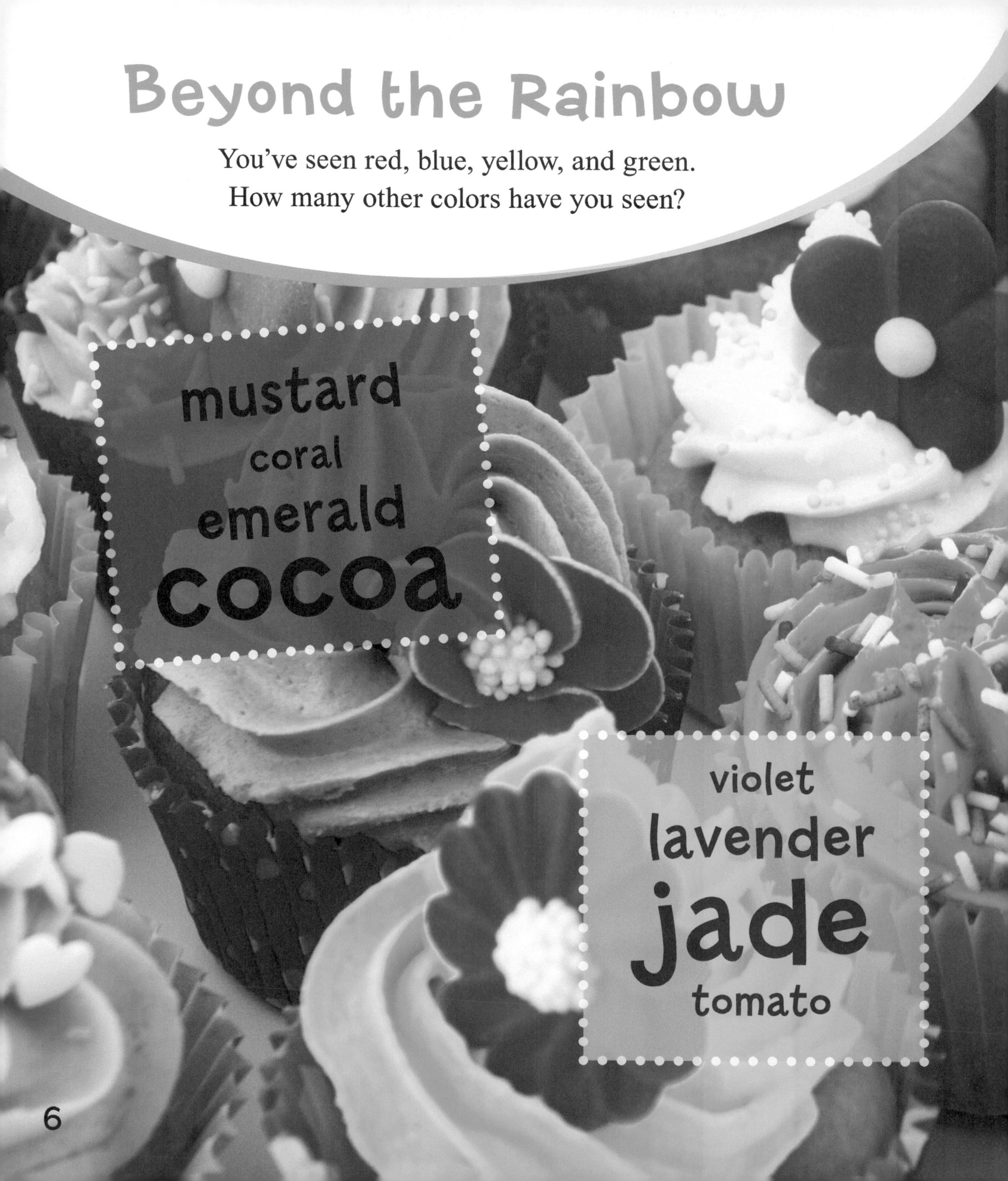

aqua
lime
cobalt
crimson
magenta
copper
turquoise
lemon

Size It Up

Super big or super small,
these fun size words will cover it all.

mammoth
colossal
jumbo
gigantic

enormous
gargantuan
massive
titanic

mini
tiny
itty-bitty
teeny
wee
petite
pint-size
teensy

How Do You Feel?

How do you feel about summer or school?
Or ice cream? Snakes? A day at the pool?

grumpy
scared
goofy
sleepy
bored
gloomy
puzzled
weepy

Your Listening Ears

Think of all the sounds you hear,
the sounds that tickle your ticklish ear.

screeching
buzzing
snapping
stuttering
humming
crying
barking
muttering

Not the Same

Opposites are different as can be.
If one bird is caged, the other is free!

wild/tame
dirty/clean
swift/slow
friendly/mean

What's Your Speed?

When you move, when you go,
are you fast, or are you slow?

speedy
rapid
supersonic
quick

hasty
zippy
snappy
brisk

poky
plodding
sluggish
crawling
lazy
tardy
shuffling
dawdling

By the Numbers

"How many?" is a question we often ask,
and these adjectives are up to the task.

twelve
eighteen
every
seven

many
one hundred
less
eleven

most

each

forty

more

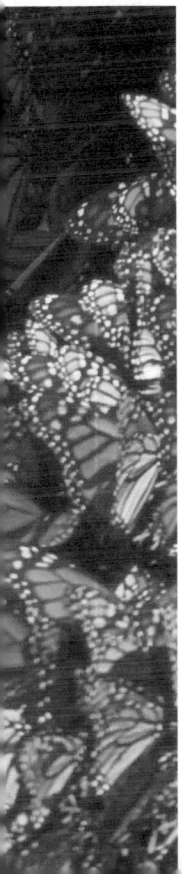

few

five

some

sixty-four

Weather Report

What will the weather bring today?
Will you need boots and mittens to play?

frosty
blazing
humid
wintry

frigid
icy
sizzling
fiery

nippy
chilly
sweltering
muggy
blistering
steaming
frozen
sunny

Who Are You?

What kind of kid are you?
Helpful? Kind? Honest and true?

brave
bubbly
wise
dramatic

generous
smart
healthy

athletic

stubborn
funny
thoughtful
brainy

bold
fearless
timid
zany

The Shape of Things

These words describe how objects look.
Which word best describes this book?

narrow
curved
straight
steep
skinny
rippled
thick
deep

Taste Test

Grab your fork, and dig right in.
So many foods, where do you begin?

mushy
chewy
bitter
pasty

sticky
rotten
crunchy
tasty

Keep in Touch

Your sense of touch helps you know
if something's hot or cold as snow.

sharp
shaggy
itchy
grimy
grubby
damp
rough
slimy

What a Day!

Was your day better than just OK?
Then try these words. They're fun to say!

awesome
amazing
remarkable
marvelous
brilliant
stupendous
splendid
fabulous

Read More

Carter, Andrew. *Adjectives.* Grammar Ray: A Graphic Guide to Grammar. New York: Alphabet Soup, 2010.

Cleary, Brian. P. *Quirky, Jerky, Extra-Perky: More about Adjectives.* Words Are Categorical. Minneapolis: Millbrook Press, 2007.

Fandel, Jennifer. *What Is an Adjective?* Parts of Speech. North Mankato, Minn.: Capstone Press, 2013.

Riggs, Kate. *Adjectives.* Grammar Basics. Mankato, Minn.: Creative Education, 2013.

Internet Sites

FactHound offers a safe, fun way to find Internet sites related to this book. All of the sites on FactHound have been researched by our staff.

Here's all you do:

Visit *www.facthound.com*

Type in this code: 9781476539379